ADVENTURES
WITHIN
ANOTHER

ADVENTURES

— Within —

Another

STORIES OF IDENTITY AND CULTURE FROM COMO PARK HIGH SCHOOL

Adventures Within Another © copyright 2017 by the authors and Mid-Continent Oceanographic Institute. All rights reserved. No part of this book may be reproduced in any form whatsoever, by photography or xerography or by any other means, by broadcast or transmission, by translation into any kind of language, nor by recording electronically or otherwise, without permission in writing from the author, except by a reviewer, who may quote brief passages in critical articles or reviews.

ISBN 13: 978-1-63489-069-4

Library of Congress Catalog Number: 2017940329
Printed in the United States of America
First Printing: 2017
21 20 19 18 17   5 4 3 2 1

Illustrations by Kelly Abeln, Greta Kotz, and Sarah Platner
Cover design and illustration by Kevin Canon
Page design and typesetting by Mayfly Design, and typeset in the Chaparral Pro typeface

www.moi-msp.org

Minneapolis, MN
www.wiseinkpub.com

To order, visit www.itascabooks.com or call 1-800-901-3480.
Reseller discounts available.

All proceeds from the sales of this book help support MOI's free programs.

CONTENTS

PLACES

THINGS

"...Hold close and remember the things that made you who you are in the story of your life."

—KAO KALIA YANG

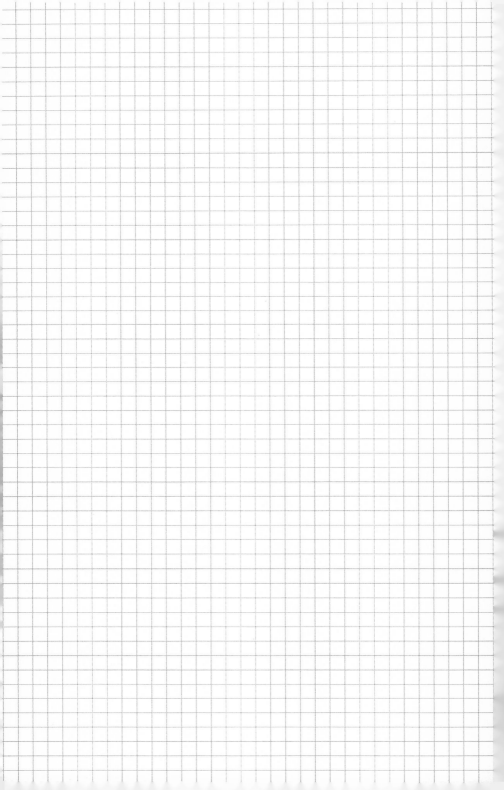

FOREWORD

Once upon a time when I was much younger, a girl closer to you than my present self, I had a cultural artifact that I cherished. It is long gone now, lost to the debris of time, but I can remember very clearly the story of how it came to me and how it kept me safe all those long, childhood nights through.

It was a token from Laos. It was perhaps the only gift I ever got from my mother's mother, a woman I never had the opportunity to meet. In fact, my own mother has spent more of her life with me than she ever did with her mother. They were separated by America's secret war in Laos long before I was born. I remember the small, crinkly plastic bag that it came in. The scent of deep earth, burnt hair, and dry medicinal herbs emanated from the plastic bag in my mother's hands. Inside, there were four little bags about the size of quarters, each in the shape of a triangle, sewn with unsteady fingers. My grandmother from Laos had sent the bags across the wide ocean to her grandchildren in America, young people she'd never met and I believe she knew she never would.

My mother had recorded a cassette tape (this is before international calls were feasible for the Hmong community that had just arrived in America) to my grandmother. In the spool of shiny black tape, my mother had told her mother about her second daughter, Kalia, me. I was a child full of fear.

Before we came to America, when we were still in Thailand preparing for the trip, I had fallen down before the dead body of a Laotian woman. I had first seen her on a visit to the camp hospital to visit my sick uncle. Her bed was right beside my uncle's. The woman was not yet dead. Flies buzzed around her still form.

Her eyes were closed but her mouth was open. She took deep, jagged breaths. Her intestines were all hanging out in a plastic cover around her belly. Something had gone terribly wrong, and it was clear to me, even then, that the woman was closer to the dead than the living. The stench of rotting flesh emanated from her. A helpless IV dripped into her bulging arm, more purple than pink or yellow. It was the warm hand of my mother under my chin that shifted my gaze away from her body. A few days after our visit, my uncle came home. We, my cousins and I, learned that she had died. Her body had been transported to the funeral shed. Anybody could go in there and take a look. It was nothing more than an open doorway into a darkened hut. The guards were more interested in guarding the living than the dead. My cousins and I decided that we would visit the woman and have a final look at her open belly. We all knew what our culture taught: if you fall before the body of the dead, the dead takes your spirit. But we were children and we felt far from death and we wanted to test out our fears, so we went, a group of seven or eight. I was the youngest. I remember the older kids running to the open doorway and peeking in and then, fleet of foot, they skipped away, hands over mouths. It was my turn. I ran as fast as I knew how over the pebbly earth. My eyes were trained on the body in the darkened shed. I did not look at my feet. I was right before her body, in the doorway, when I fell over a toppled rock. Hard and heavy. I felt the rough ground greet my chin. My older sister and my cousins scrambled to help me up, but it was too late. That night, safe in my father's arms, I saw the dead woman, no longer laying down, but standing straight up, in the corner of our sleeping unit, looking at me, breathing her heavy breath.

I came to America with a fear of the dark, a specific fear of the labored breathing that echoed from the tall body that stood in the shadowy corners away from the moonlight's glow. In the tape to my grandmother, my mother told her of my fear of the night, my inability to sleep when all else was quiet. I had not expected my grandmother to respond, but respond she did.

She sent my mother the triangle bags so that I could grow brave under their watch. She told my mother that inside each little bag was the burnt hair of a dead spirit (to show whoever meant me harm, dead or alive, that a grandmother's love knew no fears). There were ashes from the incense sticks that she had burnt to the spirits of the earth, the water, and the sky to ensure our safety, to share in her love for us. There were herbs from her garden, planted from seeds she'd collected from a lifetime, from the war-torn jungles of Laos. In each little triangle bag, my grandmother from Laos, the grandmother I had never met, sent me everything she believed could fight fear: expressions of love.

I took one of the triangle bags and I put a safety pin on it. For years, I kept it pinned to the pillows I slept on, the vehicle of my dreams. Through the long nights, across the span of seasons, as the years shifted atop each other, the triangle bag kept me safe and I grew strong with sound sleep. Somewhere along the way, the safety pin grew old and weak, and one day I lost the triangle bag that my grandmother had sent me from the ashes of memory, the reach of love across distance and time.

I no longer have my most cherished cultural artifact, but its story lives on inside of me. Today I share it with you, along with the voices of these young writers, so that you, too, can hold close and remember the things that made you who you are in the story of your life.

—KAO KALIA YANG

ACKNOWLEDGEMENTS

Mid-Continent Oceanographic Institute (MOI) launched its inaugural Young Authors' Book Project during the 2015–2016 school year to showcase the creative writing talents of two classes of Farnsworth Aerospace Magnet School fifth graders. For this second year of our publishing project, the MOI crew decided to highlight our longstanding partnership with Como Park Senior High School by partnering with two sections of Risa Cohen's ninth-grade reading classes. Over the course of six months, these ninth graders worked shoulder-to-shoulder with MOI's classroom volunteers to create a portfolio of original works discussing the people, places, and things students identified as central to their own sense of culture and identity. Our staff and volunteers are thankful for the work and candor of these incredible ninth graders.

In addition to our young authors, MOI would like to thank the dedicated volunteers, Como Park faculty and staff, student families, funders, our 826 National mentors, and the MOI staff and board members without whom this project would not be possible.

To our classroom volunteers—Julia Fritz-Endres, Courtney Overland, and ML Kenney—thank you for giving freely of your time and skills to work with students on multiple drafts and genres. Additional classroom support from MOI board chair Kathy Thomforde and board member Paul Von Drasek—as well as MOI staff members Lauren Boritzke, K. Cross, Chad Kampe, and Max Meier—helped ensure the project's success.

Many thanks to Como Park Senior High School's principal, Theresa Neal, for approving and supporting this project. To classroom teacher Risa Cohen and educational assistant Diana Schirm, thank you for allowing us to work with your students for these past six months. To Ms. Mund, we remain grateful that you allowed our students and volunteers to work unfettered in your light-filled library. To the security team of Modesto Correa, Samantha Garcia, and Carletta Perry, thank you for the many, many visitor's badges each week and for helping our volunteer corps navigate campus hallways. To Maria Cocchiarella, MOI remains indebted to you for helping us forge and maintain our working relationship with Como Park Senior High School.

To Kevin Cannon, thank you for your beautiful cover designs and section break pages. Few professionals would willingly accept real-time critique of their work from a room full of ninth graders. We deeply appreciate you walking students through the creative consultation process to craft a cover that reflects their identities and aesthetics. Local illustrators Kelly Abeln, Greta Kotz, and Sarah Platner patiently navigated shifting schedules to meet with individual students and produce unique spot art to accompany each student's work. Thank you for your generous time commitment and gorgeous finished products.

MOI is deeply grateful for the returning members of our design and publishing teams. Ryan Scheife has once again transformed our manuscript through his layout design. Dara Beevas and her Wise Ink Creative Publishing staff, including Patrick Maloney and Roseanne Cheng, were back again this year to cheer us on. Thank you all so much for the time and energy you put into making this book a resounding success for our students.

We also owe a debt of gratitude to our returning editorial volunteers who have given freely of their time (and patience) to ensure a professional end-product our students can be proud of. To Anitra Budd, Molly Hill, Laura Kaliebe, and Miriam Skurnick—thank you.

We are continuously grateful for the ongoing support of the 826 National network, which inspired and made this adventure possible, and look forward to future collaborations. From 826 National, we want to shout out the support of Gerald Richards, Kait Steele, and founding author Dave Eggers.

This project received major financial support from The Bigelow Foundation, The Saint Anthony Park Foundation, The Saint Paul Foundation, Wise Ink Creative Publishing, and MOI's individual donors to ensure students' pieces made it to print. The MOI staff would also like to thank our board members for fundraising, supporting, and actively publicizing the creation of this book.

Finally, significant thanks are owed to author Kao Kalia Yang, who graciously chose to write the foreword and speak with our student authors. Many students were deeply moved by the words she chose to share. We are honored to be a part of this master storyteller's legacy and humbled by the opportunity to share literary space with her.

On behalf of the entire board and staff of the Mid-Continent Oceanographic Institute, thank you to all of our supporters and champions. Your work makes projects like this possible.

ABOUT THIS BOOK

You are holding a compendium of original works created by Como Park Senior High School ninth graders for Young Authors' Book Project. Each piece contained inside is written by a student author who workshopped their story side by side with volunteers and staff from the educational nonprofit Mid-Continent Oceanographic Institute (MOI). Students, teachers, volunteers, and staff worked together in the classroom for six months to compose the stories you are about to read. A talented team of illustrators, designers, editors, and publishers volunteered to help bring our finished product to life.

Inside you will find both poetry and prose that detail the people, places, and things students consider reflective of their identity and communities. In keeping with the spirit of MOI's mission, students were given creative license to share the stories they feel are most critical. We asked simple questions to jump-start students in each of the different styles. Throughout their writing, many students described important people in their lives, from secret crushes to loved ones who have passed away. These poignant stories fill our "people" section. Our young writers then crafted pieces for our "places" section in response to the prompt, "What do you hear when you think of home?" We began the year together by asking students and volunteers to bring in a cultural artifact identifying them with a particular community. Many of their resulting stories can be found in the "things" section. The title, cover, and individual illustrations accompanying each student's piece were all selected in close consultation with this year's young writers.

We encourage you to turn the page and join our young authors as they take you on an *Adventure Within Another*.

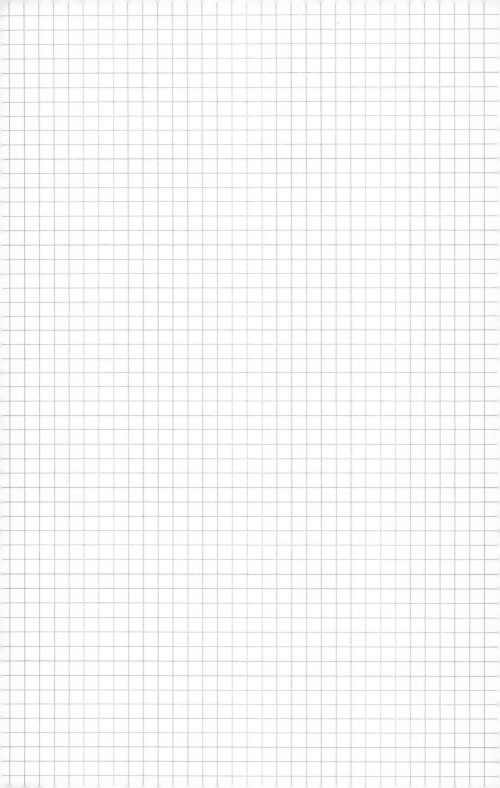

PEOPLE

I AM NOT A TERRORIST

Hawi Ali

I am Muslim
Not a terrorist

I'm a Muslim girl
No, I am not a terrorist
So think twice before you judge me, brother
I'm just a human being like you
With different beliefs and culture

I was born and raised in Islam
Believing one God
Who is Allah
I believe Islam means Peace

But social media has warped how people think
With assumed terrorism tearing my family apart
Mom from her son,
Son from his mom
Tearing apart
People trying to make their country a safe place

But all this started because of people who would assume all
   Muslims are bad

It started with slavery
People taking control of what wasn't theirs

Showing me the fake side of them
Making me believe
Those smiles are real but all they do is
Go behind my back and
Kill my people

Sorry that I'm a little protective
But I'm not a terrorist
I'm not telling you to love me, brother
Just think twice before you judge me

Love comes later,
Brother

LITTLE BORDER BIRD

Zak Bricker

Little border bird, why don't you fly away?
I don't fly away.
I don't have anywhere to go.

While I sat there watching the trains fight with their language
    of horns and whistles,
I hid in the background
But I was always caught even when I was in the most impossible
    spot.

I ran multiple times.
I always came back.
Eventually I asked the trains, "Why do you guys fight?"
They looked at me with their mightiest stare.
They said, "We aren't fighting, little bird, we are speaking loudly
    to fix our differences."
That was the last I heard from that train.

The very next day, I didn't hear the normal morning yelling.
I looked at the yard.
To my dismay, I saw only one train.
It appeared lost and depressed.
I searched for the other one but couldn't find him anywhere.

I scoured the entire train yard.
I asked the other trains
They gave me the same dumb answer, "No."
Eventually I gave up and returned to the lonely one.

When I arrived at the yard, she seemed happy and joyful.
This strange action of her for him missing baffled me.
I was confused, but the sight of her made me feel happy.
So I stayed with the one train, feeling safe and secured.

Why, little border bird, don't I fly home?
I don't fly,
And I don't need a home.

Why?
Wherever I go with her,
I'll always be home.

SECOND CHANCE FOR LOVE

Faye Patricia N. Cea

We are everything to each other
Our love is like a treasure

We had been waiting forever
To finally be together

We still have feelings
And yet you're leaving

You say you've found someone new
But she doesn't know you like I do

She doesn't love you like I do
She doesn't care like I do

I believe you will come back to me
Our love is meant to be

How long will you make me wait
To recover from my heartache?

My heart needs a shield
Cause love is a battlefield

Faye Patricia N. Cea lives with their parents. Their favorite sport is volleyball, which they began playing in ninth grade and still play to this day. When Faye Patricia and their family were living in the Philippines, they were on a championship volleyball team. They studied mathematics at a college before moving to the United States, and now want to pursue engineering.

CIGARS

Leonce Corder-Campbell

As I smell the tobacco from the cigar
I remember my uncle
My uncle Sid

He used to smoke a lot of cigars
The tobacco had the very strong scent of burning wood
Every time I smelled it, it would burn my nose
The cigars would start making me cough
Then I would run outside
While my uncle was making a hotbox
Even when I was outside I could still smell it

Some days he and I would go to the park
He would smoke some more cigars
Maybe three to five Black & Milds
They had a white tip with a black wrapper
Four inches long and the size of your pinky

The other kids would look at him
They would whisper in their ears
Point and laugh at me
Even though many other people smoke at the park.
He would sometimes embarrass me

He told me not to smoke cigars or cigarettes
I promised him I wouldn't

He was really, really wise
He was the type of guy who would know a lot of intelligent people
Like Malcolm X
All the presidents
Shakespeare
He would also tell stories of what not to do in life
He regretted doing many of the things he told me
The choices that he made when he was a young man
He would tell me to not make these mistakes that he made

I promised him I wouldn't . . .

BOYS & GIRLS

Eunice Gamino-Barragan

As little girls
we all said:
"We hate boys!"
"Boys have cooties."
As little girls
We only trusted
each other with
Our secrets and
Our lives.

Now that we are older
Boys seem different:
They could be friends,
They could be more,
Who changed?
Did we?
Did they?
Does it matter?

The future holds
More Possibilities
More relationships
Than we once thought
When we were little.

Boys and girls,
don't be afraid of each other.
We're more the same than different
We can trust each other with our secrets and our lives.

* * *

Eunice Gamino-Barragan lives with their mom, dad, and little brother. Their favorite food is Mexican food like posole. In their free time, they like to read, sing, color, walk, and sleep.

I WONDER IF...

IDIL HASSAN

I wonder if everyone goes to bed at night,
Not wondering whether they'll see their family again.
Never wondering if they'll ever wake up.
Believing that this life is endless,
Blind to the most obvious signs.
But...

What if I'm not prepared,
Not prepared to leave?
To leave this life for the afterlife.

Well, I was told no one is,

I was told to live life.
And afterlife will be taken care of.

IF YOU WERE HERE WITH ME...

Reebar Htoo

I wish you were here.
I wish you'd never left.
But mostly, I wish you well.

I wish you my very, very best.
It hurt so much to let go.

Remember the shirt you gave me during December?
I held it to my empty heart
while tears started to fall.

The teardrops that have been falling
will soon open my heart and
I will know that I will have to stand alone.

Know that you are still with me in my heart.

I never knew you would
play with my feelings.

Maybe all of this is an experiment
that I can learn from.

What is love?

Every night I wonder
What is love?

What did I do for you to leave?

I imagine a little angel above me.
Wishing that the broken heart was
all a sad dream.

Not only did you leave me heartbroken,
but you left a scar.
A scar that is not repairable
but is a constant reminder of you.

The fairy tale that I once knew is gone.
All of the memories will fade away.
The stormy days will pass.

Soon the sun will rise
and the rainbow will show once again.

* * *

Reebar Htoo identifies with the Karen community and enjoys writing. They feel that the way their writing comes out accurately expresses the best of them and their feelings. Reebar has also enjoyed playing since they were little.

ALL THE LIES I TOLD MY TEACHER

ELIJAH JOVEL

All the lies I told my teacher,
Because of her disrespect.
Teachers piss me off so much
I barely get time to reflect.
But a student can't tell them anything
without them getting upset.
She likes to yell,
I'm not the one who starts.
I tell her one thing
and she takes it straight to the heart.
I want to show her how I feel, maybe she should become a
    student and I a teacher.
I'm the type to skip her class, and my excuse would be me
    getting a seizure.
My teacher made me write this poem
about all the lies I told my teacher.

MY HAIR

Kortney Killion

I am black with
    beautiful hair

I am black with beautiful hair.

They say, "You look like Krusty the Clown."
Is it because my hair is in a fro?
Is it because I'm black?

They say, "Looks like you got electrocuted."
They say, "What's wrong with your hair?"

When I look in the mirror, I look fine.
My hair is fine and beautiful
Just the way it is
It styles itself

You think you hurt me
But u make me stronger

Your words hurt but
U won't break me

I am black with beautiful hair.

FRIENDS

POR LOR

In the cafeteria my friends and I are laughing
I see my friends' smiles

One of the guys is switching his voice
From high to low
High and squeaky like a little bird
Low as an old man

After the last bell we go outside
Sprinting around the soccer field
Hand reaches to a shoulder

You're it!

* * *

Por Lor lives with their grandpa and grandma. Their favorite sports are basketball, badminton, and flag football. Por's favorite way to spend a Saturday is playing video games.

SHE HAS MY HEART

Chit Koe Nai

When I'm around my crush, my stomach starts to hurt and my
    heart falls in love.

I see her face sometimes in my dream, hard to reach.
I see her everywhere.

When I touch her, I feel like I'm in love with her.
When she talks to me, I feel like I'm in a dream.
I feel like I'm in a dream.
When I'm talking to her, I feel like I'm intruding on her
When she is with her friends or family.

If I'm being honest with you . . .

When the sky is blue, you know I'm thinking of you.

I'm fascinated when I look at you so dreamily.

I feel like I'm in love with you.

Don't pinch me when I look at you.
I don't want to lose daylight daydreaming about you
For no reason.

Love doesn't end when I'm with you.
It feels like a butterfly in my stomach.

I just want another kiss from your lips.

I feel right now as I never felt before.
What I see in you I totally adore.
What I want right now: a kiss in front of your house door
And to have you by my side when I'm in trouble.
To calm me down.

I promise our love will be the best, so promise me,
between you and I, our love will be the best.

Guys like me think about you every second.
Guys like me work out to catch your eye or feeling.
Guys like me run just to catch you.
That's why l love to the end.

My life didn't start with you,
but I want it to end it with you.

●　●　●

Chit Koe Nai enjoys playing *Just Cause 3* on PS4. For the most
part, they can be found sleeping, especially on Saturdays.

MY DAD...

Paw Say

I can't tell you, Daddy, how many tears
I've cried. Since the day I was told,
my precious dad had died.

You never said you were leaving,
you never said goodbye.
You were gone before I knew it,
and only God knew why.

It seems so impossible, although I know it's true, as everything
I see around,
it reminds me of you. A million times
I needed you,
a million times I cried.

If love alone could have saved you,
you never would have died.
I can still hear your laughter
and see your smiling face.

I would have lost my sanity if not
for God's saving grace.
In life I loved you dearly.
In death I love you still.

In my heart you hold a place
that no one could ever fill.
It broke my heart to lose you,
but you didn't go alone.

For part of me went with you
the day God took you.
I didn't tell you this often enough,
but I really love you.

I love you, Dad,

and want you to know how I feel your love wherever I go.
Whenever I've got problems, you're there to assist.
The ways you have helped me would make quite a list.
Your wisdom and knowledge
have shown me the way,
and I'm thankful for you as I live day by day.
I didn't tell you enough how important you are.
In my universe, you're a bright shining star.

You're such an important person in my life.
I have to close this letter now,
but this is not goodbye.
For you will forever be with me in my heart and mind.

MY DAD

Andrew Shorty

My dad was my everything.
I loved him to death.
He passed away April 24, 2014.
I thought it would never happen.
I thought he would never leave.
I was heated!
I'll say it again.
I...was...so...damn...heated.
I had so many thoughts. I even asked myself why.
Then I started to feel like death was part of life.
My aunt called. She asked where I was.
I told her, "On my way home."
She said, "OK" and hung up the phone.

◉　◉　◉

Andrew Shorty's favorite food is nachos because they are messy.
Their favorite sports are football and soccer. They are a part of
the Como Park Senior High School robotics team.

A STUFFED BEAR FULL OF HEART

TRINITY ANN MARIE

Two years ago, I was lying in a bleak room in a sort of uncomfortable hospital bed. I heard the machines of monsters beeping at me, giving me IV fluids and insulin drip, and I was just told I'm diabetic.

One day, I was finally moved to the diabetic floor, and the door opened and a "bag of hope" came through. My crystal-blue drained eyes locked on the honey golden brown bear named Rufus.

This bear had eyes as black as coal, and he was dressed in Juvenile Diabetes Research Foundation (JDRF) clothes. I noticed there were patches of different colors all over his body for different places that I could give myself insulin shots. He was soft like silk at the touch, like the feeling when you touch something and you don't want to stop. By the time I locked my eyes, my tired ones, on Rufus, I finally could breathe without a worry. In some way Rufus was my protection, my security, even though he was just a stuffed bear.

I was released from my monsters of wires and my cage of a room, and the pain of the cold medication in my arm, and the noises of my heart sighing on the machine in that stressful situation because I was taken to the "floor of the stars."

My stepmom took me from the floor of intense medical attention. I had Rufus in my hand. I slowly walked along the halls of the vibrant color-flashing stars. My newly freed and bruised hand felt the plastic stars on the wall. Then, my eyes opened widely and I smiled. The stars sang to me as a quartet.

Rufus has been around since 1996 and has brought joy to everyone around him. There are many bears that are like Rufus, but the bear I have is special to me in so many ways. Rufus may not talk, but he sure can listen. He may not physically be alive, but he sure is a good shoulder to cry on. He may be full of stuffing yet he has a heart of gold in my eyes. Rufus has been there through thick and thin, and I can't wait to keep him throughout my diabetic journey. If I ever get trapped back in the monster machines and locked in a cage of medical attention, I know Rufus will be there with me.

❋   ❋   ❋

Trinity Ann Marie is 14 years old and began writing at a young age. They wrote down all the memories they had when they lived on the East Side in addition to the ones made when they moved to the Como area. Trinity wrote about their journey with diabetes and believes their JDRF Crew would be happy to hear it.

BEHIND A SMILE

WAH WAH

People say, sticks and stones may break my bones
But words will never hurt me
The truth is, they do.

We hide the pain we feel inside
We cover up our emotions with laughter and jokes
We go to music, poetry, or for a walk
Just to forget about our problems for a while

At the end of the day those feelings come back

They visit us, hunt us

"I was joking."
"I didn't mean what I said."
The truth is:
There's always a truth behind a little lie
A cry behind a big smile
Everyone has feelings
Nobody is perfect

We've avoided our problems so much that sometimes we feel numb
We feel like no one would understand us
No one feels the way we feel

No one would fall in love with us

Sometimes hiding away from the world is the only solution
Late at night, while others sleep, we stay awake.

So awake that we can hear every sound our heart beats
The sound of how worried we are
The fear of not being good enough,
Failing,
Letting our loved ones down.
Sometimes a little emotion is okay
But sometimes it takes over our mind and we forget
How to function in the real world

WITH YOU

PHILLIP YANG

I'd rather have
Bad times with you
Than good times
With someone else.

I'd rather be beside you
In a storm than
Hide inside
Safe and warm.

I'd rather be struck
By lightning snow
Than redirect
And see you go.

I'd rather blow away
In wind and rain
With you than hide away
In a basement, sane.

I'd rather have
Hard times together
Through arguments and weather
Than to have it easy apart.

* * *

Phillip likes to play both volleyball and football. In the future, they plan on getting into the photography business. Phillip's favorite food is cinnamon rolls because they are sweet and soft to eat.

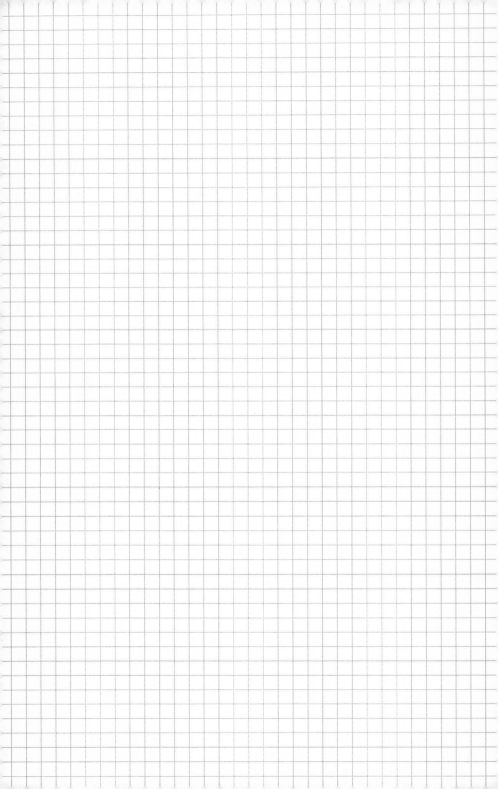

PLACES

2009

A. KEH

When I was seven years old
When I came to America
When we were really, really happy
When everyone in our family felt happy and sad at the same time
When we were blessed . . . we really were
When it was my first time living in an apartment
When we were mice stampeding to broomstick on the
ceiling . . . hahahahaha
When everywhere felt like the '50s . . . it really did
When kids' TV shows looked vintage . . . it really brings back
memories
When Cookie Jar TV, CW4Kids, PBS Kids, and Qubo were my jam
When we celebrated our first Christmas in America
When "sorry" was my first English word . . . I think . . . or was it "hi"?
When I actually had a mind of my own . . . and I did a lot of crazy
stuff
When I was always outside having fun . . . because I didn't have
curfew
When I was really energetic . . . I really was, my family would be
really strict about everything having to be clean and orga-
nized haahahahahahahahh
. . . to be honest it's
When my life finally started beginning

When I started taking control of my life
When I actually had a mind of my own
When I was alert
When I wasn't in the house 24/7
When I loved the outdoors
When I had a really nice teacher
When school was actually fun
When school was about learning instead of passing
When we had recess every day
When I started speaking English
When I loved making friends with people because they weren't fake
When there were no temporary people in my life
When I felt like I was free to do anything
When I used to have a good voice
When I had music class every day in school
When there was actually a choir
When I learned how to swim
When I learned how to ride a bike
When all the good songs came out
When my life was happy

● ● ●

A. Keh's favorite sport is soccer because it is a sport they are actually good at. They spend their Saturdays watching movies or entire TV series on Netflix. A. Keh's favorite food is pho because it is delicious and everyone should try it.

WHERE I'M FROM

KTRU MOO

I am from where the rice is grown,
The weather is fresh, under the feet.
I'm from under a leaf, blanket, and covers,
Smiling face and fire burnt the candle.
I'm from where birds flew away to settle.
Like a seed under soil that needs water.
I'm from this little hand can pray,
And faith lead us like water.

I'm from houses, not a home, and crawling with feeling.
I'm from eight lives, eight minds,
Eight hearts and smiles.
I'm from "don't sing while you eat"
Or the tiger eats you.
I'm from the wind singing, leaf dancing,
And "things don't last forever."

I'm from under a roof but not under a roof,
And even permanent marker doesn't last.
I'm from Hill Tribe house, made of bamboo,
Dirt, leaves, and smoke flying.
I'm from spicy food, wheat fields, green forest,
And strong root.

I'm from looking up at the moon, wishing on a star,
And moving on.

My family is like a watered flower.
When the flower is grown it becomes lovely, beautiful,
And it feels special like a dead tree still growing.
We are a blast of brightness,
To know it is a blessing from God,
Whether we are close or far,
We are a family in love like moon and star love each other.

* * *

Ktru has a cat named Grey. They live with their parents and enjoy playing soccer.

TRIPS THROUGH THE OCEAN

ANISA SMITH

Orcas Island on a ferry
Kayaking in the ocean
Waves crashing
Feel the warmth of the sun
Sea lions, eagles, turkey vultures
Jellyfish, starfish
Sea lions gliding under the water
Salt water on my hands
Crashing through waves
Every island paddled by
Really cool

● ◉ ●

Anisa Smith loves hanging out with friends and family over the
weekend. They live with their mom, dad, and two siblings. Their
favorite sports to play are volleyball and hockey.

WHAT I HEARD

SOE R.

I heard my friends talking about playing at the park.
I went to play with them.
We were planning to go to the park together.
There were dogs barking.
My friends made a big soccer team
And I joined them.
We played until sunset, listening to cars driving by.
We went home together, ate some rice, and
I went to my room to sleep.

I heard my brother playing a video game in his room,
People cheering when they scored.
I went into his room.
He said, "Come join me."
He said, "Let's play together,"
And I joined him.
It was fun
Playing the soccer game with my brother.
It was Saturday, we were playing pop music on my brother's phone.
We played video games and listened to music until nighttime and
We played all we wanted
And then we went to sleep.

I heard my sister laughing outside and
I went to the door to see what she was laughing at.
She was sledding down the hill with my little brother
And they were having fun together.
I heard a squirrel squeaking in the tree.
My sister told me to sled with them,
And I joined them.
So I went inside to get a winter suit.
I heard people talking on the TV.

Talking family and friends,
Playing soccer at the park,
Pop music on the radio.
Playing with my friends and family
creates the sound of fun.

* * *

Soe R. plays soccer for Como Park Senior High School. In fact, they can be found playing most Saturdays. They live in St. Paul.

CALM POEM

DELEELA ROBINSON

Calm, positive energy
I hear myself being Zen
I hear no worries in the world
I hear myself breathing
Listening to the wind whisper calming things
Everything is good
Everything is calm
Everything is positive
Everything is quiet
Everything is Zen

* * *

Deleela Robinson lives in the Midway area near Hamline Park. They are really into sports such as volleyball and soccer. They are also really interested in photography. Deleela really likes expressing how they feel through the pictures they take.

HARD TO CHANGE

CHER THAO

Fall comes
I walk out of my house
walking on the sidewalk

On a lonely day
I see leaves falling around me,
on the ground, road,
and sidewalk
I see a tree without a single leaf

I hear the cold wind whisper to me,
softly crying like a lonely wolf howling
leaves dancing along the wind
the leaves feel the sadness

Mom's meal tastes bitter

All the things I see,
feel, taste, and hear,
all start to fade away

WHAT I HEAR

SNAY T.

The white back door squeaks slightly.
I finally made it home. I hear
My family talking about life
Paying bills,
going shopping,
three stories of squeaky stairs.
My brother plays video games,
double-couch, gun shooting,
light-polluted, car racing,
People shouting out the window,
Footsteps on top of us, rhythms below us
Ceiling floor wall window door sounds
These are the sounds I hear every day,
this is the world I live in.

● ● ●

Snay T. lives with their two brothers, one sister, and parents in a
house. Their favorite food is Asian food. Snay likes to play PS4 on
Saturdays.

WHEN I THINK OF HOME

Ger

When I think of home
I hear a lot of arguments.
I hear a lot of other noises
refrigerator and freezer humming
shutting doors,
fighting, shooting, racing from the video games.
Kids running around
sounds of the sink and bath
when the waters are coming down.

When I think of home
I see me playing with my friends
we would play in the playground.
We played tag
played hide and seek
especially at night
we would hide under cars
behind bushes
we've hidden higher up on trees
so that the leaves will cover us.

When I think of home
I see myself punished for secretly riding bikes in the street

and doing dangerous things
we would ride bikes around the block
sometimes off to stores not too far away.

When I think of home
I see my family and our life now
I also see my childhood.

＊　＊　＊

Ger has been living with their parents since they were born.
They like football, basketball, and video games, and even played
on their middle school football and basketball teams. In the future, Ger plans on being an engineer because they like math and
hands-on activities.

SECRET WORLD

Payai Vang

There is always a secret world in everybody's eyes
A world of many things that we outside may
Never know
A world where they cried to themselves
A world where they think about negative thoughts
A world where no one else will understand
A world when there's no one to trust
They will only believe themselves
A world where they thought about doing stupid things
A world where they wanted to escape
A world that they wish
To not look back
Ignore all the things that they've done
A world where they want to keep it a
Secret
A world when nobody can figure it out
A world that is like a puzzle to everyone outside

HOME

Savoyah Broadway

When I think of the word home
I hear laughing
When I think of the word home
I hear my mom singing throwbacks
And it bugs me, my mom can't sing!
When I think of the word home
I hear peace
When I think of the word home while I'm in school
I get happy
Impatient
Excited
When I think of the word home
I think of sleeping & eating my favorite things
Cereal, noodles, snacks, or whatever I found
When I think of the word home
I think of my bed
Oh how comfortable it is
How fast I'll fall asleep.

THINGS

FOOTBALL

CAELAN

I went to an NFL game with my friends and cousins a couple of years ago. It was a Vikings vs. Green Bay game, and we all got some food from the concession stand. We sat in the middle row along midfield. My friends Cam, Darjon, Damon, and Jarnell were betting that we could catch a football at kickoff since there was no net around the field. I thought we were too short, so we started to chill and watch the game. Then we said, "Let's go to the front seats so we can catch the ball." Some of us went to the bottom row, closest to the field, and the kicker kicked it off. The ball bounced off the ground and landed in this person's hand who was sitting in front of me. He dropped it, I caught it, and the person said, "Hey, his seat's not down here!" so we ran off, ran out of the stadium, with the ball.

The football is real leather and it has an NFL logo embossed on the side. It sits in my room on a glass stand on top of my desk where I can see it every day. I don't play with my game ball because it is valuable and it's going to be worth a lot of money someday. It's the same football professional players use in the NFL. I like to look at it because I want to be a football player in the future. I've wanted to play football since I was seven years old, and I now play for both of my high school's junior varsity and varsity teams.

My football looks like a classic NFL ball with white laces and dark brown leather. The football I got at the NFL game feels nice and smells and looks like it's been played with. It's dirty and all beaten up. My friends and I want to play football through college and for the rest of our lives. We want to be like our favorite NFL players and on our favorite team. We made a promise that we will become pro NFL players after I caught the game ball. The moment was awesome, and every time I see my ball on my desk, I think about our promise to go pro and the great time we had at the game.

* * *

Caelan has two dogs, a pit and a rott, and their favorite food is pasta because of the flavor. Their favorite sports are football and basketball.

COMMUNITY ARTIFACT

Abdifatah Daoud

My community artifact is my purple soccer jersey that has the number seven on the back. The front proudly displays the name of our sponsor and says, "Fly Emirates." Emirates is an airline that supports my soccer team, Dawa. Emirates represents the Somali community. "Emirates supports Somalis" is printed next to the logo. My soccer team members are all from the Somali community, and they are all different ages, from teenagers to adults. I got my soccer jersey last year after I tried out for this Minnesota community soccer team. Being on the team was good exercise for me instead of being at my house playing video games. I enjoyed being on the team because I made a lot of new friends.

In the game that decided whether or not Dawa would play for the Minnesota State Cup, I was fouled in the penalty box. I was going for the ball that my teammate had short-passed to me when a player from the other team kicked me in the right knee. The referee called for a penalty kick while the other team yelled that it wasn't fair for me to get a penalty kick since their player hadn't gotten a card. I told the referee, "I am going to kick it." My teammates didn't want me to take the shot and thought I would miss. The referee signaled, and I sank the ball into the upper-left ninety of the goal. The yellow net stretched all the way out from the power of my shot. Dawa wound up winning the game 3–0.

In the next few weeks, we had a big game coming up, so the coach told us that we had to go practice from 8:00 p.m. to 9:00 p.m. I wore my jersey to the practice that night. In the middle of practice, I got injured because another player kicked me hard in the leg. I limped off to the sideline and called my parents to take me to the hospital. I had to go to the doctor from 8:45 p.m. to 10:00 p.m. I was still wearing my jersey, but the doctor told me to take it off. The doctor said I couldn't play anymore. I said, "Okay." That night I washed my jersey and thought about how my team would need me to play in the tournament. I had to play or we were going to lose the State Cup.

I played center striker for my team during the State Cup final. We won, but I did not score any goals. It wound up being my last game of the season. My soccer shirt has four stars that represent the last soccer World Cup and reminds me of how hard my own team works all the time. I still wear this article when I am playing soccer with my friends. It is important to me to show everyone that I was a part of a community one time. Dawa means "watch my skills," but to me the team meant family.

❀   ❀   ❀

Abdifatah Daoud likes pizza because it is yummy and the slices each have a triangle shape. Triangles are the best shape. On Saturdays he likes to go on adventures to the Mall of America, which is exciting because it is intimidating. Abdifatah identifies with the Somali Community.

MY CHICAGO CUBS JERSEY

ALEX

Twelve years ago, my dad gave me a Chicago Cubs jersey. It is gray with blue letters that are outlined in white. My dad originally got the jersey from my grandma, but he was moving this year, so he gave it back to my grandma because he didn't have any room for it. And so when I was at my grandma's in October and she was going through some clothes and asked if I wanted it, I said sure. I choose not to wear the jersey a lot because I don't want it to get dirty or ripped and it's only for special events like watching Cubs games.

My dad has had the jersey since I was two or three, and I remember seeing him wear it every time he watched the Cubs play. The jersey is in almost perfect condition, except for a couple stains from cheesy pretzels, hot dogs, and Mountain Dew that my dad would have in the living room while watching the Cubs play. On November 2nd I was up until 11:46 pm watching game seven of the World Series. It was the Cubs going up against the Cleveland Indians. It was a really close game until the eighth inning. The Indians tied the game up 6–6 in the bottom of the inning when Rajai Davis hit a two-run home run over the left field wall.

I started getting really stressed out and anxious because it had been a really long time since the Cubs had been to the World Series, let alone won one. The last time the Cubs won a World Series was in 1908, but ever since 1908 there has been a curse. Since 1908, Cubs fans have feared the Curse of the Billy Goat, the Bartman Curse, the Curse of the Black Cat, the Babe Ruth's

Called Shot Curse, and the Prior/Wood Curse. Fans would use these curses to explain why every time the Cubs would be in a World Series game they would lose.

During the 2016 World Series, I had a weird feeling in my stomach because the game was in extra innings and it was the top of the tenth inning and the Cubs and Indians were still tied 6–6. The Cubs had the meat of their order up, and three of the four people got on base. Montero was up with two outs and two people on base and the count was 3–2. It was a perfect pitch down the middle. He hit it down the third baseline and it rolled into left field. Rizzo started running really hard from second, Zobrist started hustling from first, and they both scored, giving the Cubs an 8–6 lead in the tenth.

Now it was the bottom of the tenth and Edwards was on the mound facing Cleveland's best hitters. He walked one guy and retired two other people, but the Cleveland player who tied the game up in the eighth, Rajai Davis, was up. Edwards overthrew a ball, and the person on first stole second. Rajai Davis then got a base hit up the middle, getting an RBI from the person on second. The score was now 8–7. Edwards took a couple of deep breaths and threw the last pitch of the game. The batter hit a grounder to Kris Bryant, the third baseman, and he made an off-balance throw to Anthony Rizzo, the first baseman. Bryant had to release the ball quickly to get the runner out, and he did. He threw out Lindor, and the Cubs won the World Series. After 108 years, the Cubs finally broke the curse. Everyone in my house was asleep, so I couldn't scream loudly. I put a pillow up to my face and yelled happily in the living room.

My jersey is really important because my dad's whole side of the family are die-hard Cubs fans. They have been waiting so long for the Cubs to be in a World Series and finally win and be world champions. My grandma went to a lot of Cubs games when she was younger and living in Chicago. She bought the jersey at a home game, and when my dad was old enough to understand the game of baseball, she passed it on to him. My dad kept the jersey until he moved to a place where he didn't have enough room for it. Then he gave it back to my grandma, who kept it at her house in one of the spare bedroom closets. The reason my family loves baseball so much is because my grandpa used to play a lot as a kid, so he taught my uncle and dad how to play baseball. They turned out to be really good, but my dad and uncle stopped playing after high school. When I was six, my dad signed me up for T-ball in 2007 to see if I would like that sport. I loved it. I've been playing for nine years in a row. My dad tells me that I really loved the sport, so after I played a year of T-ball, my parents said I wanted to move right up to coach pitch.

In 2008 I started my first year of coach pitch. All I remember is having so much fun and loving to have people actually throw a ball to me. My dad said I was improving big time and he wanted me to play kid pitch. I was unsure about it, but I thought, and I wanted to play kid pitch. So after coach pitch was over, I moved right up to my first year of kid pitch in 2009. As I moved up, I really wasn't expecting kids to be that good and I didn't realize that kids would pitch as fast as they did for their age. I didn't really like playing kid pitch because I couldn't hit the ball. I was really upset because I thought it would be easier than it was. I practiced with my dad every day at our old house to get better. Now I play competitive AA baseball for Shoreview, and I was ranked sixth best player in the league in 2016.

●　●　●

Alex is the owner of an eleven-year-old yellow lab. During their free time, they enjoy playing baseball outside and also NBA 2K17. Alex lives with their mom and little brother in a medium-sized house near Hamline University.

NECKLACE SEALED IN LOVE

Abreya Hensen

Two hearts, gold and glitter.
Gift to a favorite granddaughter,
Gift given from one heart to another.
Only worn to special events, two hearts of love they represent.
To my birthday and to fancy parties it is worn.
He gave it to me when I was first born,
I was still little, he came to the hospital.
I was a baby, like really small, it didn't fit at all.

He showed me his love and his commitment.
As I grew older so did our bond.
Didn't see him for a while, but then he moved nearby.
His job as a grandpa is to love me, give me money, take me places
Till I get grown, then I can give him money and take him places.
Given to me to mark that I'm his first and only daughter's child,
Two hearts, gold and glitter.

SEALED IN LOVE.

* * *

Abreya Hensen lives with their blind uncle, and their favorite food is pizza because of the shape. On Saturdays, Abreya can be found sleeping, eating, and partying.

THE BLUE PAPER

WAY RAYMOO HTOO

My eighth-grade honor roll certificate is important to me because I earned it through hard work. It has my name in the middle to recognize me in big, black, bold letters. The certificate has my principal's and counselor's names on it so people know who gave it to me. My certificate is blue for B honor roll students. The yellow ones are for A–honor roll students. My certificate is as big as a piece of paper in a notebook (8 ½ x 11 inches) but thicker. The certificate is from Battle Creek Middle School. The school gave it to everyone who got straight As or Bs.

You can use a certificate to show people that you are a responsible and respectful student. You can show it off to your parents and friends and they will be very proud. My parents were really proud of me when I showed them my honor roll, and they were happy. I want them to smile and say nice things about it. I am proud of myself too. The honor roll is really important to me because I work really hard on it by doing all my work and staying on track with what I'm supposed to do. The honor roll certificate represents that I'm a good student.

The purpose of the certificate is to prove that you're a hard worker and you respect other people. You can be a role model to other students. The outcome of being on the honor roll is that I can help people who are in need of help. I know I can help other people because if I can earn that certificate, I can help them too.

My teacher's purpose is to inspire me to do all my work even if it's hard. They expect me to at least try and give everything I've got to earn it. You will achieve your goal once you know what you want to do. You can learn a lot of things when you get your honor roll certificate. You can learn that you're a good student. I learned that by doing my work, I can achieve good grades. By getting good grades I will prepare myself for college, a job like a detective, and a good future.

* * *

Way Raymoo Htoo loves pizza rolls because they are the best; they find them absolutely irresistible. Way also enjoys attending youth group meetings where the staff helps with homework and are always friendly and helpful. In the future, Way wants to become a detective and solve cases.

MORE THAN JUST A SHIRT

LORI MILIAN

My choir shirt is red and has big white letters stating CCC (Chicago Children's Choir). It is used to represent our choir and the teams that make up the whole. Its purpose is for recognition and as a token of respect. It's a size medium V-neck. It has a hole in the bottom from the time my friend and I got into an argument about the correct way to pronounce a word from a song. She stabbed me with a pencil and it went through the shirt. Every time I look at it, that hole reminds me of her, the choir, and my accomplishments in it. I got the shirt from the director. You are given this shirt once you are promoted from CCC to 3-Dimensions. This shirt is made of cotton that seems to be really soft and comfortable to me, bringing even more value. CCC is the starter group; once you've gained experience, you will be promoted to 3-Dimensions.

Looking at the shirt reminds me of places I went with my choir and of my favorite choir director, Mr. Bruno. He was the most flamboyant, corny person I ever met, but that's what made me like him even more. He took time out to actually teach us the lyrics and their meanings if they were in another language. He always pushed me to sing and to lead my team to the best of our abilities. After he left, I never gave up on my team because that was the only thing he ever talked about. Whenever I was feeling like I couldn't do it, he always pulled me aside and said, "There is no *I* in team, but there is an *m* and an *e*," and, "Think to yourself, don't leadership and achievements start with me?" That shirt is a symbol of success, pride, and our achievements.

The shirt reminds me of the time another student and I were being promoted. All of us had to wear the red shirt, and the directors had to wear their uniforms. As I looked around, it made me feel as if everyone was there just to support me and the other student, which they were. But it made me feel even more proud. And the look that my best friend was giving me made me feel as if I was really serving a purpose to the choir. But without the shirt I still felt as if the kids looked up to me for direction and guidance. That was the purpose I was there to serve.

*   *   *

Lori Milian loves to dance, whether it is goofy or for real. Their Saturdays consist of either adventuring out or being on their phone. When Lori is older, they want to be a police officer.

A SYMBOL OF FRIENDSHIP

October Paw

One of my favorite gifts I ever received was from my best friend, Emma. She gave me a necklace made of silver. The medallion part is a little smaller than a dime, blue, and it sparkles. The chain has beading around the neckline. I got it on my fourteenth birthday.

The necklace reminds me of Emma, whom I met in middle school and am friends with to this day. When I first saw her, we didn't talk, but one of my friends, Abby, introduced us. Emma and I then started having conversations. She was very kind and thoughtful. We share what we have in common and we laugh a lot together. My best memory of Emma was when we went on a school trip to a camp called Wolf Ridge. We went canoeing on the lake and we hiked together. Another favorite memory of Emma took place on my fourteenth birthday. We were at my friend's house, and I didn't know that they were going to surprise me. Emma gave me the necklace in a gold box with a bow on it.

When I wear the necklace, it reminds me of Emma and what a special friend she is. Necklaces go back to the earliest people in history. They would be made in different styles with bones, shells, and teeth. Early humans wore them as decoration and as a way to communicate. Necklaces represent wealth, power, relationships, identity, and status. They all have meaning. For me, my necklace means friendship, and Emma.

● ● ●

October Paw lives with their parents and siblings. Their favorite food is pizza because, plain and simple, pizza rocks. October's favorite sport is soccer.

MY CELEBRATION:
HMONG CULTURE CLOTH

LUE

Something important to me is a cloth made from fabric and string that was made by my parents. This cloth was made before my parents were married. The background color is black and there are green squares. It is small, like the size of a kid. It was made in Thailand, and I received it when my family first moved to St. Paul, Minnesota.

My culture cloth is used for special celebrations like Hmong New Year and church. It is important in our community because it represents our culture and who we are. The people in the Hmong community would feel like it's a good thing to tell people about our culture. It means that the Hmong culture won't be forgotten. Every family's culture cloth is passed down generation to generation to pass on our culture.

My family's cloth commemorates the past when something bad or good happened, such as when someone passed away or when it was a good day to celebrate. Every family uses the same artifact, but it is a different color. The cloth changes to have lots of different colors. It is also modified to have more than one type of fabric, such as Hmong cloth with pennies hanging on it. There's also Hmong cloth that girls wear, which has a hat that comes with it.

My culture cloth is used to get into different types of celebration. My favorite time was when my family and I went to the New Year celebration in Fresno, California. At Fresno New Year, my family and I went and ate at a restaurant where the tables were outside and there were lots of people. During the celebration, we were wearing our personal cloths. I'm excited to celebrate Hmong New Year every year.

* * *

One of Lue's favorite foods is spaghetti because of the tomato sauce on top, and their favorite sport is soccer. On Saturdays, Lue likes to eat a large meal with their entire family and celebrate birthdays.

MY RINGS

KEVIN VANG

My rings were a gold color, and they have faded into a bronze color. I wear these rings around my ring finger on my left hand, set on top of one another. My rings are thin and smooth, but the color on the bottom of my rings tarnished from gold to bronze, and now they leave a blue stain where they are placed. My girlfriend, Anna, bought me the two rings. I bought her a ring that is a silver color with a diamond. I bought her rings at Icing, and she bought mine from the same place. We bought each other rings after we had been dating for five months.

Anna moved from Detroit, Michigan, to Brooklyn Center, Minnesota, when she was only three or four years old. My cousin Samantha introduced me to her through a dance community called Iny Asian Dance Theater (IADT) where Anna also danced with my cousin. I asked Anna if she would want to go watch my movie that I acted in with me. She hesitated, then she said yes. We hung out a lot before I asked her to come watch the movie I played in. I thought Anna could relate to the movie, *1985*, because it talked about the Hmong community coming from Thailand to Minnesota. Anna, who is also Hmong, had to move to Minnesota from her home in Detroit. During the movie, I finally gained the courage and asked her, "Would you be my girlfriend?" She didn't bother to give it a second thought and she said yes. Our rings symbolize that no matter how far apart we are, love will always hold us together. We are still able to see each other about every two weeks. She told me to never lose my rings, and I said the same.

My rings mean a lot to me. They give me a reason to try harder than my best. They keep me safe because even if she isn't here, I am reminded that she's still with me through my rings. Her ring means: "I wear it to keep me company, make me feel safe and secure, and that your presence is always here with me." It holds us close even when she's so far away.

* * *

Kevin Vang lives with their birth mother and stepmother. They are the second oldest in their family and love dogs. Sadly, Kevin's dog passed away after a hit-and-run. Their favorite food is Chinese food.

COIN BELTS

Juliet Xiong

Coin belts are made out of mixed colored clothes sewn together with different colored cloth, coins, and beads hanging around. My coin belts are thirteen inches wide and fourteen inches long. They have Hmong symbols on them that stand for safeguards against ill fortune. They have two circles curled on each side that are connected to each other. We wear them during New Year's Eve once a year to honor and preserve our ancestors.

Hmong people historically harvest all the foods they have left before New Year's Eve. They then share all their harvested food and love for the Hmong people, showing that we are a family of Hmong tradition. We love each other.

Most men wear coin belts, which have bright colors with elaborate patterns and elegant coin works. Hmong people make them by hand. Most adults use bigger coins to adorn their embroideries. Hmong families have enthusiastically continued and preserved these artistic traditions, which have been passed down from generation to generation.

I feel special, beautiful, and lucky when I wear a coin belt on New Year's Eve because Hmong women traditionally wear them. I feel much older, mature, and respectful. I love to hear the coins jingle around lightly and see the colors lighting up brightly every time I wear a coin belt.

MY BLUE JROTC T-SHIRT

KEVIN YANG

JROTC is my favorite class because we do fun activities like physical training. If you don't know what JROTC stands for, it's Junior Reserve Officer Training Corps. I have friends in that class, and we all wear the JROTC shirt every Friday. It's blue and has a bulldog on the back. The bulldog represents the Marines because it's their mascot. I got it on the first day of school, and it's a size medium.

We use our shirts when we do community service to represent Como Park Senior High School JROTC. Our school represents the Marines, and we are the only school that does. Washington High School, a nearby school, represents the Navy SEALs. We got our shirts for working at the State Fair, where we picked up trash and helped others.

Everybody in JROTC has to wear it on Fridays. Every year it changes colors. Last year it was red and it was a National Guard shirt.

● ● ●

Kevin Yang lives in St. Paul, MN. They like to fish for bass and play football on Saturdays. They also like to sleep and go outside if it is nice.

FREE FOR ALL

L. YANG

Playing CoD on a spree
like there ain't no stopping me.
Also horse, on the court,
from outside a jump shot three.

But I never hit a shot.
All they do is drop shot
Like standing under hoop
And handing me a pot shot.

They think they all that
Time to bring out the LSAT
Their jaws drop when
I half-court sink that

With the Intervention in FFA,
I QS at game point I TS.
When we shoot we don't play like DS
I yell E when I see you miss.

Spray and pray
Got sweat on my palms
Staying calm
I seize the day

Playing online, I don't get tired.
But beating you on the court has me wired.

CoD = Call of Duty | FFA = Free for All | DS = Nintendo DS
QS = Quick Scope | TS = Trick Shot | LSAT = A Specific Light Machine Gun

* * *

L. Yang lives with their parents, siblings, and uncle. Their favorite sport is basketball and they also like playing video games. L. Yang also likes to listen to Logic, their favorite rapper.

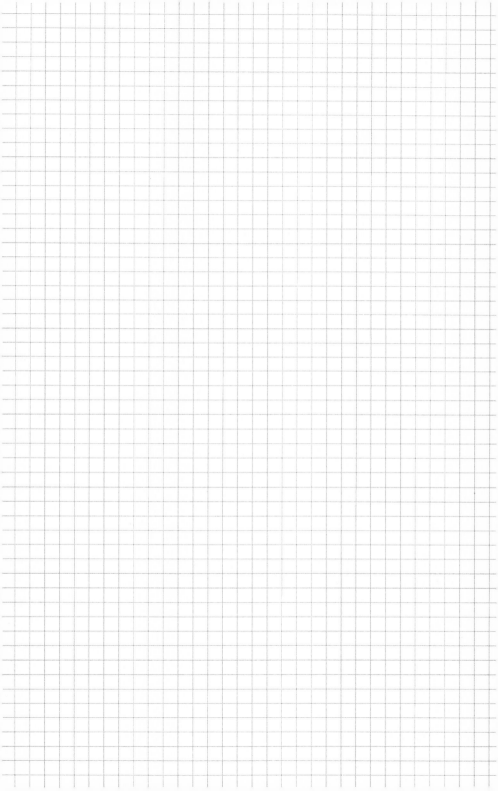

ABOUT THE SCHOOL

Como Park Senior High School serves over 1,300 students in grades 9–12. The high school is part of Minnesota's largest public school district, Saint Paul Public Schools. The school's mission is "To provide a rich learning environment that challenges and supports all students in finding and developing their own gifts and continuing the journey to reach their potential." Como Park students live out the Cougar's motto to "Belong, Explore, Achieve, and Succeed Together" every day.

Students attending Como benefit from a variety of academic and extracurricular options. The Advanced Placement program offers more courses than any other Saint Paul high school and students from across the district can elect to attend Como's Academy of Finance (AoF). The AoF track prepares students for careers in business and finance through a combination of coursework and local internships. Students can also join one of Como's decorated athletics teams, performance ensembles, or its award-winning Junior Reserve Officer Training Corps (JROTC) program. Additional student-led clubs, such as robotics, are also available.

ABOUT THE TEACHER

Risa Cohen chose teaching as a second career when her children became more independent. She returned to the classroom as a student and completed her M.Ed. at the University of Minnesota in English Education in 2004 and the Reading Licensure program seven years later. She has taught English and Reading at the high school level for fifteen years.

In the opening circle conversation of this book project, Risa joined her students, Diana Schirm, and the MOI staff and volunteers and shared an object that was meaningful to her: a quilt she had pieced and stitched together during her pregnancy with her eldest son. As she explained in the essay she wrote as an example for her students, quilt making has been a labor of love and necessity, an art, a community project, a tradition, and a way to bring comfort and hope to people throughout our country's history. She believes that teaching serves similar purposes and requires patience, skill, and dedication. Throughout the writing of this book, she has guided and encouraged her students to explore their experiences and express their feelings and thoughts in writing. They have collaborated in an artistic process that in its design represents the individuals and community of Como Park Senior High School.

ABOUT THE ILLUSTRATORS

KEVIN CANNON, *cover design and section break pages*

Kevin Cannon's illustrations and maps have appeared in the *Village Voice*, *Miami New Times*, *Minnesota Monthly*, and the *Star Tribune*, among other publications. Kevin has illustrated numerous children's books, including *Ben and Lucy Play Pond Hockey* and *Charley the Bulldog's Fantastic Fruit Stand*. He lives in Minneapolis.

KELLY ABELN, *"People" spot art*

Kelly Abeln works from her South Minneapolis studio on a variety of illustration and design projects for clients. She also creates products for her online shop, paints, experiments in her sketchbook, dabbles in pattern design and makes lists of all the other things she wants to do. See her work at: www.kellyabeln.com.

SARAH PLATNER, *"Places" spot art*

Sarah Platner attended the University of Wisconsin–Madison and the Fashion Institute of Technology in New York. She is currently based in Minneapolis working as a textile designer. When she's not busy bringing the creatures of her imagination to life you can find her exploring the outdoors, enjoying a good cheese plate and dreaming of one day owning an alpaca.

GRETA KOTZ, *"Things" spot art*

Greta Kotz is a multimedia artist from Minneapolis that has been recognized by the Society of Illustrators and Hi-Fructose Magazine. She draws with paint, pixels and paper cuts. See more of her work at greta-kotz.com.

ABOUT MID-CONTINENT OCEANOGRAPHIC INSTITUTE

Mid-Continent Oceanographic Institute (MOI) is a nonprofit organization dedicated to supporting students ages six to eighteen with their writing skills and homework, emphasizing cross-curricular creativity. According to best-selling author Dave Eggers, "Mid-Continent Oceanographic Institute is a place where the pure, unadulterated weirdness of kids is honored and amplified." In a state consistently reporting one of the largest educational opportunity gaps between racial groups in the country, we strive to echo the ethos of the 826 National network by creating a place where no student's idea is too weird, too outlandish, or too off-topic to be explored. We set this accepting tone through our own name and whimsical tutoring space. Our oceanographic branding helps us destigmatize academic support programs, hook volunteers, and promote deep dives into the creative process. MOI seeks to inspire, cultivate, and broadcast students' creativity through the following programs:

AFTER-SCHOOL HOMEWORK HELP: This flagship program serves nearly one hundred students, K–12, per semester. Hosted four days a week, we pair volunteer tutors one-on-one with students to offer academic support across all subjects.

STORYTELLING AND BOOKMAKING FIELD TRIPS: Available to second-through fourth-grade classes across the Twin Cities, our field trips strive to embolden our next generation of writers to explore and value their own voice. Students and teachers join us to craft original narratives as a class. Volunteers, including an illustrator, work with student authors to publish a book within two hours.

IN-SCHOOL TUTORING: MOI partners with Twin Cities schools to connect trained volunteers with classrooms seeking additional one-on-one support for students. Our partner school programs vary annually based on need and are open to K–12 classes.

CREATIVE WRITING WORKSHOPS: Each writing workshop represents a collaboration between student authors, volunteers, and community partners working to create original pieces around a given theme or activity.

YOUNG AUTHORS' BOOK PROJECT: In our newest program, classroom teachers, volunteers, and MOI staff work together to support students in the creative process of writing original works around a theme. Illustrators, designers, publishers, and printers, many of who offer their expertise for free, collaborate with students to create a professionally published anthology of their work.

* * *

All MOI programs are indebted to the volunteers and community partners who support them. We are honored to be invited into the schools, classrooms, and lives of the teachers, families, and students we serve. If you or someone you know has spotted the Lost Ocean of Minnesota, or cares to join us and our students in the search, please be in touch.